AI AROUND THE WORLD

EXPLORING GLOBAL USES OF ARTIFICIAL INTELLIGENCE

by Tammy Enz

CAPSTONE PRESS
a capstone imprint

Published by Capstone Press, an imprint of Capstone
1710 Roe Crest Drive, North Mankato, Minnesota 56003
capstonepub.com

Library of Congress Cataloging-in-Publication Data is available on the Library of Congress website.

ISBN: 9798875253843 (hardcover)
ISBN: 9798875253799 (paperback)
ISBN: 9798875253805 (ebook PDF)

Summary: Artificial intelligence isn't just changing lives in one country—it's transforming the world! From robotic farmers in Japan to AI-powered wildlife conservation in Africa, explore how AI is solving problems and creating opportunities across the globe. Discover how different industries, countries, and cultures use AI in surprising ways, including in medicine, agriculture, disaster response, and environmental protection.

Editorial Credits:
Editor: Donald Lemke; Designer: Bobbie Nuytten; Media Researcher: Svetlana Zhurkin; Production Specialist: Whitney Schaefer

Image Credits:
Getty Images: FG Trade, 5, 29, MB Photography, 14 (middle), RuslanDashinsky, 4; NASA: 27; Shutterstock: Andrey_Popov, 10, Applepy, 23, Asianet-Pakistan, 7, Benny Marty, 14 (bottom), Best-Backgrounds, cover and throughout (computer code), 13 (inset), CC7, 21, Craigvan184, 15, Dima Zel, 24, Gorodenkoff, 13 (computers), Hakinmhan, 25 (laptop), Have a nice day Photo, 28, Leonid Sorokin, 18, Margot Petrowski, 17, Marion Smith-Byers, 12, metamorworks, cover (middle), 22, Monkey Business Images, 11, MudaCom, 19, Nazarii_Neshcherenskyi, 25 (black hole), Paralaxis, 16, Scharfsinn, 20, SkillUp, cover (top) and throughout, thinkhubstudio, 8, Triff, 26, Westock Productions, 6, Zapp2Photo, 9

Printed in the United States 6781

Table of Contents

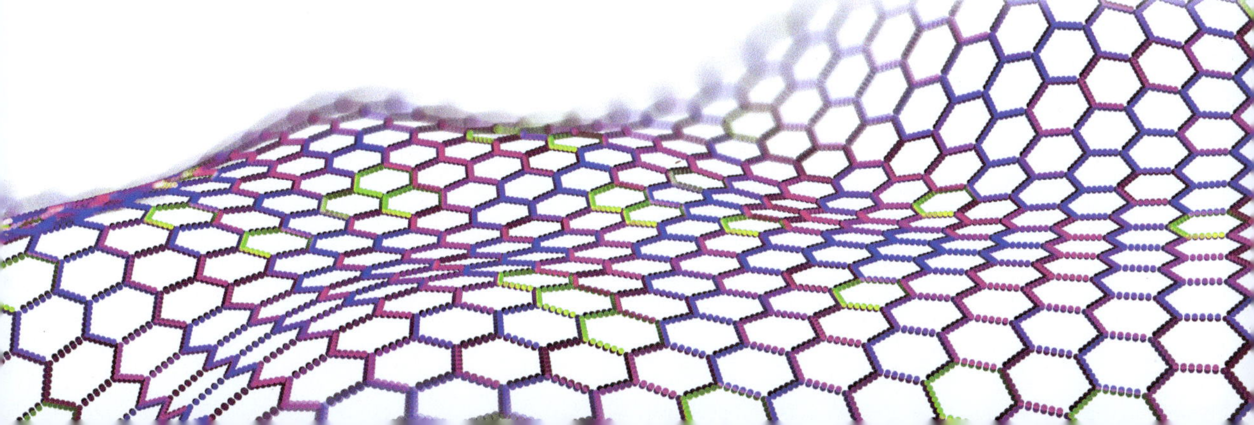

CHAPTER 1

AI and You

What is AI? AI stands for Artificial Intelligence. It's when technology—like computers, apps, or robots—can learn and solve problems. AI collects information, called data, and learns from patterns and experiences, just like you do in school. The more AI works, the better it becomes at its tasks.

Even if we don't always see it, AI is all around us. This tech helps power the tools we use around the world every day—from smart assistants to space robots.

Be Smart About AI: Check Sources

- Ask, "Where did this information come from?"
- Make sure any information is from a source you know and trust.
- Remember: Just because AI sounds supersmart doesn't mean it's always correct!

Imagine living in a small village where there are few teachers or books nearby. How would you learn? In some parts of the world, AI helps kids get an education—even when their schools are far away.

In rural parts of India, students can't always attend class. But with AI-powered programs, kids learn reading, math, and more using a computer or tablet. AI technology adjusts lessons for each learner's needs and even teaches in their native languages.

AI doesn't replace teachers, but it can support them. The technology often makes lessons more interactive by using games or videos. It gives teachers tools to reach every student.

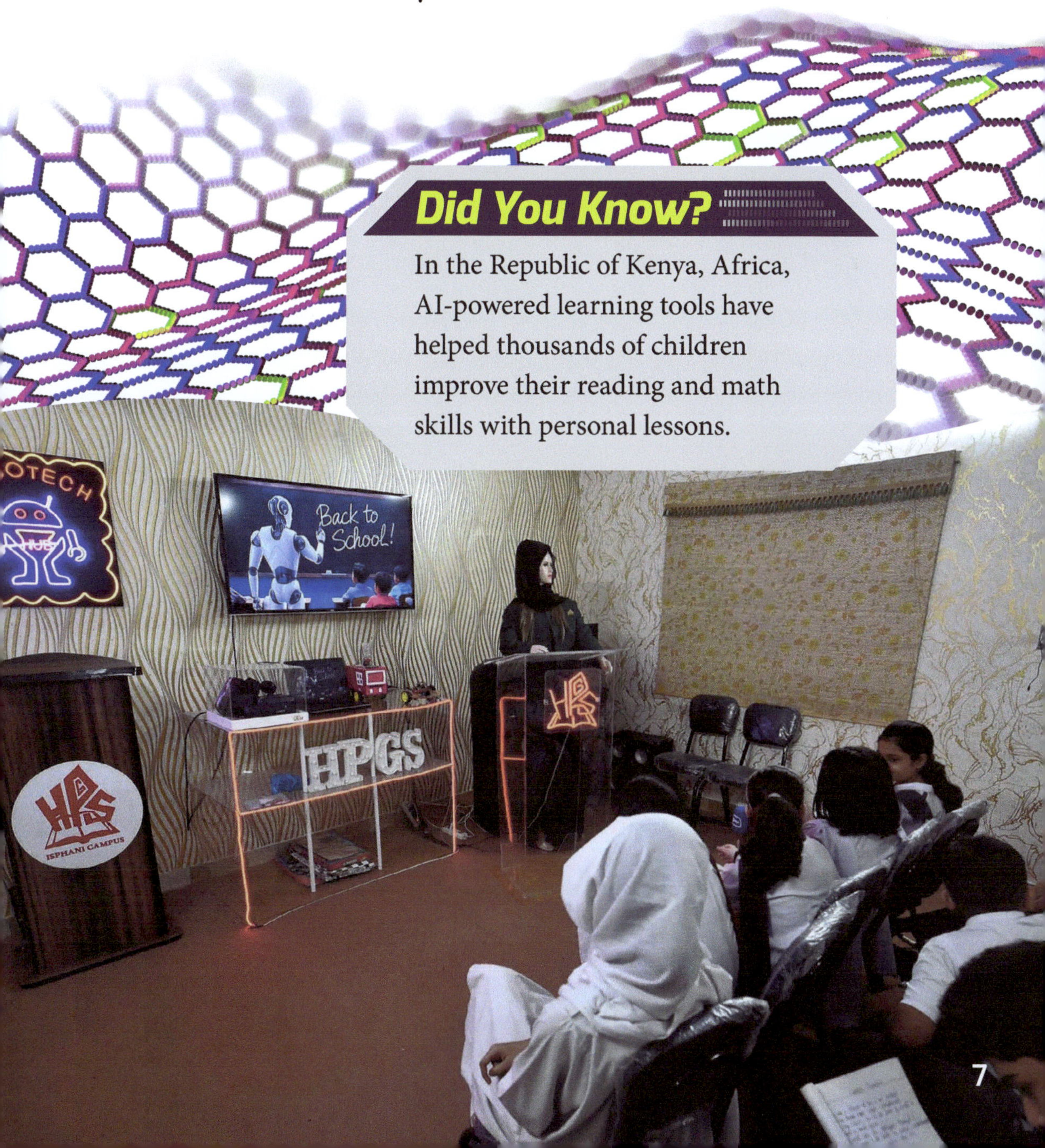

Did You Know?

In the Republic of Kenya, Africa, AI-powered learning tools have helped thousands of children improve their reading and math skills with personal lessons.

AI is also improving healthcare around the world. Doctors and nurses use AI technology to diagnose illnesses and find new treatments.

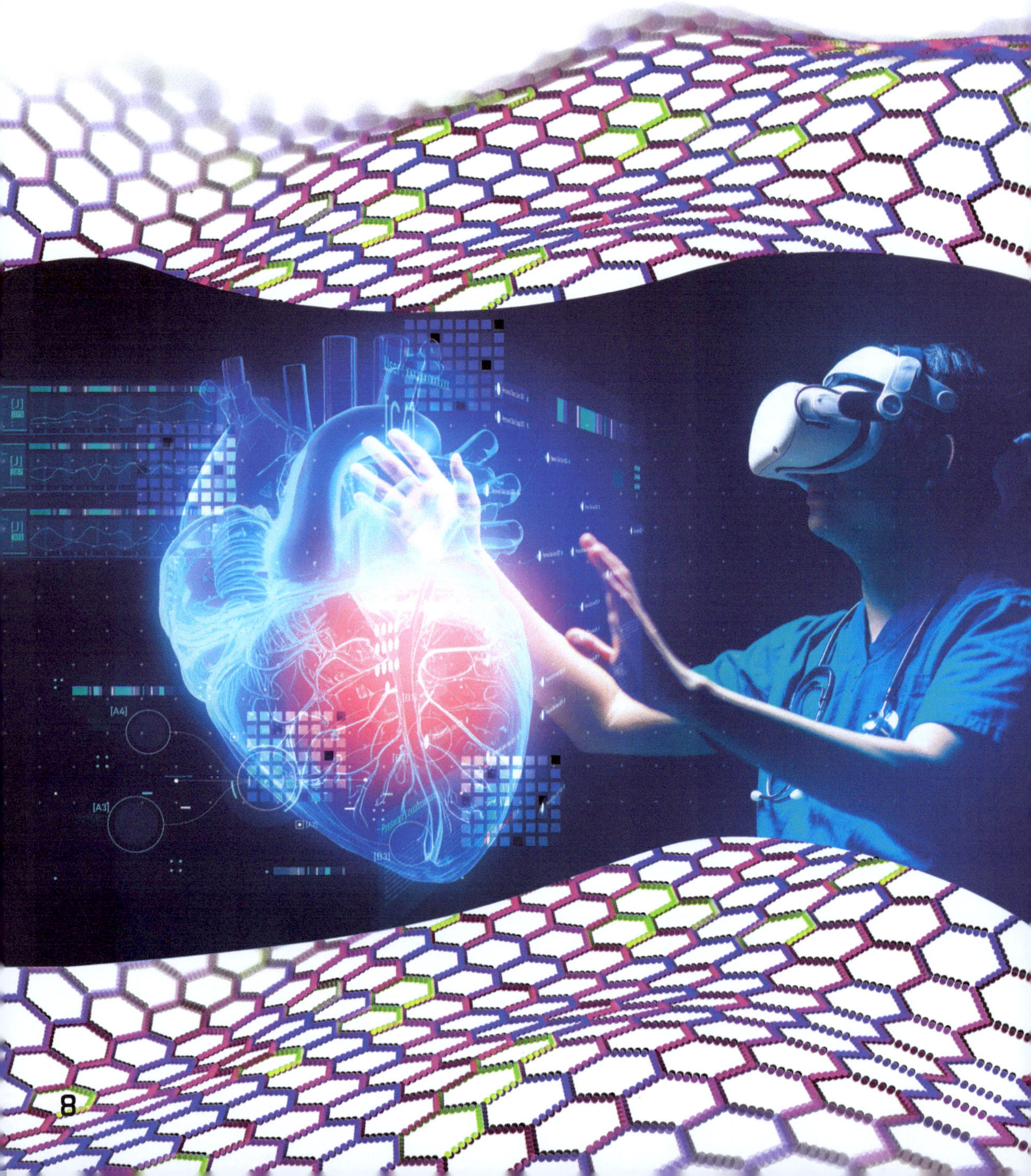

In places with few medical workers, AI can review X-rays or scans to detect problems, like early signs of cancer. The technology can help doctors figure out what's wrong—even when answers are hard to find.

Still, AI technology isn't perfect. It can make mistakes, so medical professionals must always double-check AI results.

Did You Know?

In some hospitals, AI analyzes X-rays up to 60 times faster than humans!

All around the globe, AI-powered apps track health stats, like heart rate, sleep, and exercise. These tools remind people to take medicine or get some rest.

When doctors are far away, AI can even ask patients questions about their symptoms and suggest treatments for illnesses, such as colds or stomachaches. The technology helps people get care faster, especially in remote areas.

How AI Helps in Healthcare

- Spots illnesses early by scanning X-rays and other images
- Predicts future health problems so doctors can help sooner
- Takes notes for doctors so they can spend more time with patients
- Listens to coughs and guesses what might be wrong
- Sends appointment reminders to help people stay on schedule
- Chats about feelings to help people with mental health

CHAPTER 2

AI and the Environment

AI is helping to protect endangered animals around the world. In Africa, AI-powered cameras monitor elephants, rhinos, and other threatened species. These cameras can identify specific animals by their skin patterns or the shape of their ears.

The technology also alerts rangers when it detects nearby poachers—people who illegally hunt animals. Those warnings give rangers a better chance to stop poachers before they harm threatened species.

AI technology can even scan satellite images to see where animal habitats are disappearing, helping protect those places before it's too late.

AI helps scientists track animals in oceans, forests, and deserts. It can count animal populations by studying photos and videos, helping experts figure out which species are in danger.

AI technology also records migration patterns, where animals move throughout the year. This information lets researchers plan safe routes and protect natural habitats.

Did You Know?

In Kenya, 50 rangers patrol more than 3,000 square miles (7,700 square kilometers) of elephant habitat. AI helps them track animals and stop poachers more effectively.

AI technology is helping stop illegal deforestation in places like the Amazon rainforest. Satellites powered by AI can detect tree-cutting in real time. That information is shared with local authorities, who can act fast to stop it.

AI also tracks how much energy homes and businesses use. It can help people cut down on wasted energy by showing where to save heat or electricity.

Be Smart About AI: Watch for Fairness

- Ask, "Is this fair to everyone?"
- Remember: AI can be biased or leave out important perspectives.
- Look for information from different points of view.

In many parts of the world, AI technology protects our air and water. In China, AI monitors air pollution and alerts people when it's unsafe to go outside. It also helps scientists plan better ways to clean the air.

Did You Know?

In Chennai, India, high-tech AI-powered barriers removed 22,000 tons (20,000 metric tons) of garbage from a river in just one year.

In India, AI has helped locate pollution in rivers and guide cleanup efforts. AI can even recommend better ways to prevent pollution in the first place.

CHAPTER 3

From Farm to City

Farmers in the United States, India, and parts of Africa use AI to grow more food with fewer resources. AI helps them decide the best times to plant, water, and harvest crops. It can even predict weather and reduce the need for fertilizers or pesticides.

Some farmers use robots powered by AI to pick their fruits and vegetables. These high-tech tools save time and help feed more people.

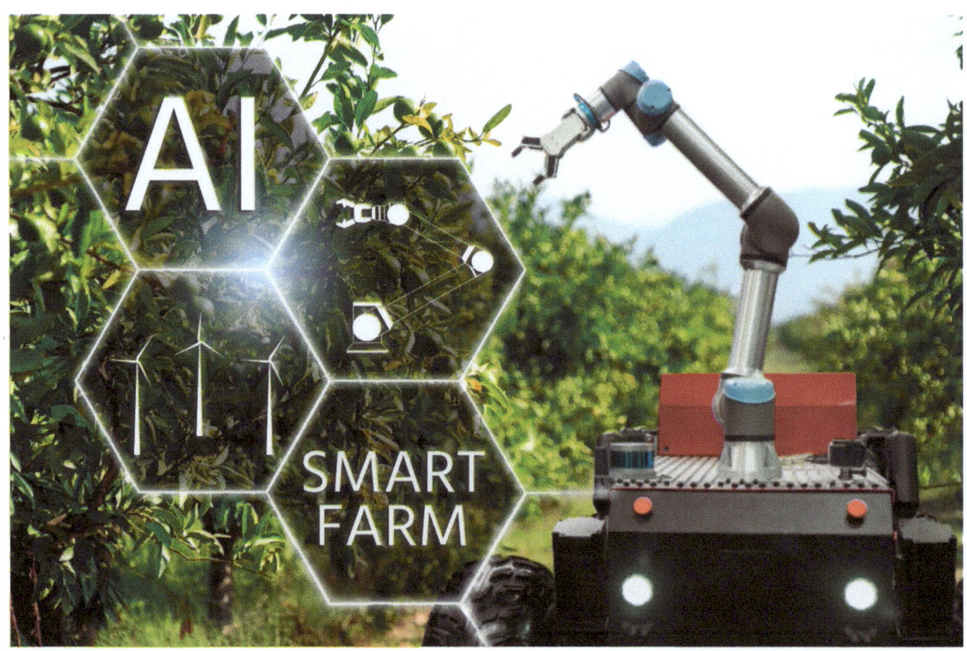

AI also allows farmers to better prepare for the effects of climate change. High-tech apps predict weather patterns and provide advanced warnings of droughts and floods.

Did You Know?

In California's Napa Valley, AI-powered robots scan grapevines and share real-time data about crop health with growers.

Cities around the world are becoming smarter with the help of AI. In places like Tokyo, Japan, and Los Angeles, California, AI helps manage traffic and keep streets safer. It controls traffic lights, finds better routes, and reduces pollution from cars.

Some cities even have self-driving cars powered by AI technology. These cars can drive themselves, avoid crashes, and follow traffic laws.

AI also supports public transportation systems. It helps buses and trains stay on schedule, so people can get to where they need to go on time.

Did You Know?

In Pittsburgh, Pennsylvania, an AI system reduced traffic delays by over 25 percent. This saved time and cut down on pollution.

CHAPTER 4

Above and Beyond

AI technology is reaching beyond Earth and into deep space. Scientists use AI to explore planets, stars, and other galaxies.

AI helps space telescopes like the Hubble and the James Webb collect and analyze huge amounts of data. It can even model black holes and distant stars to help scientists understand how they form.

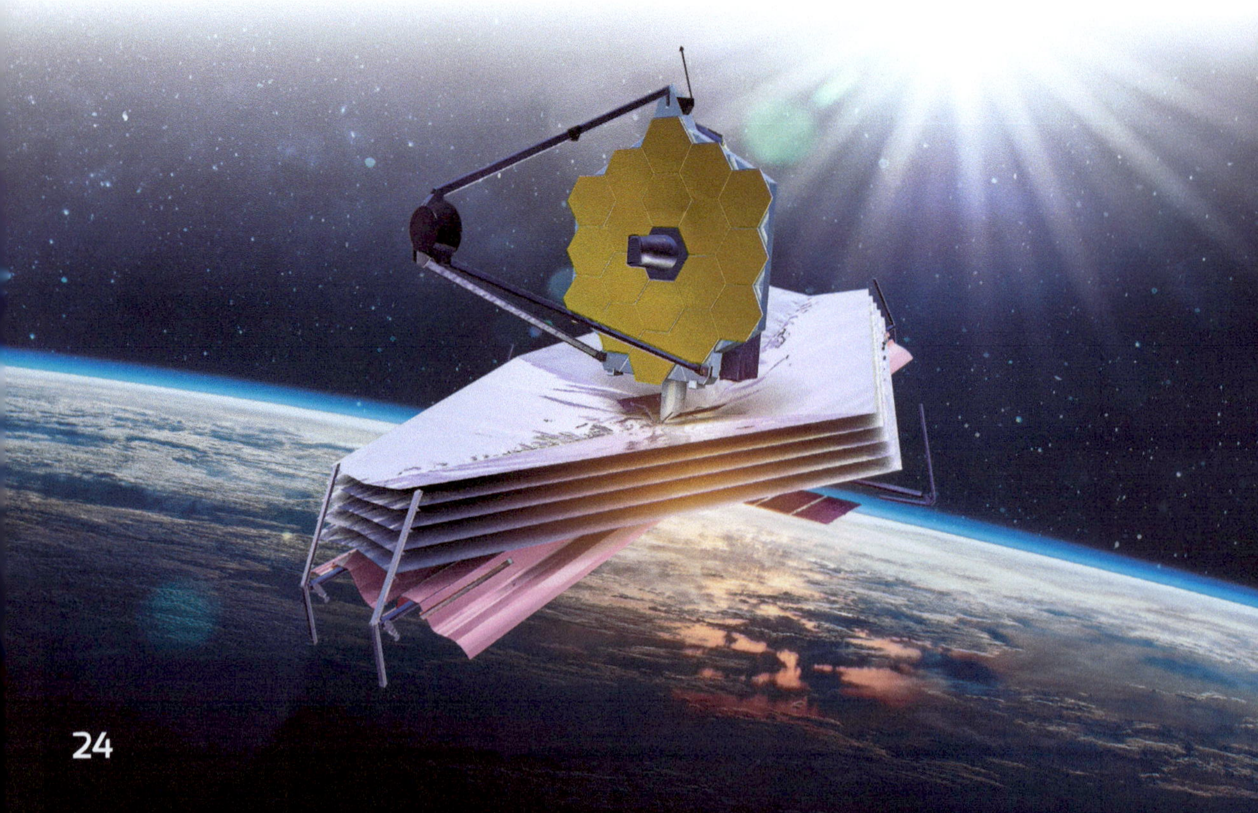

Instead of waiting millions of years to study space events, scientists can use AI to learn faster and make new discoveries.

AI is used to help robots explore space. On Mars, AI powers rovers that take pictures, study rocks, and drive themselves across the surface.

Astronauts on the International Space Station use AI to track their health, manage supplies, and fix problems on board. AI also checks oxygen levels and helps keep everything running smoothly.

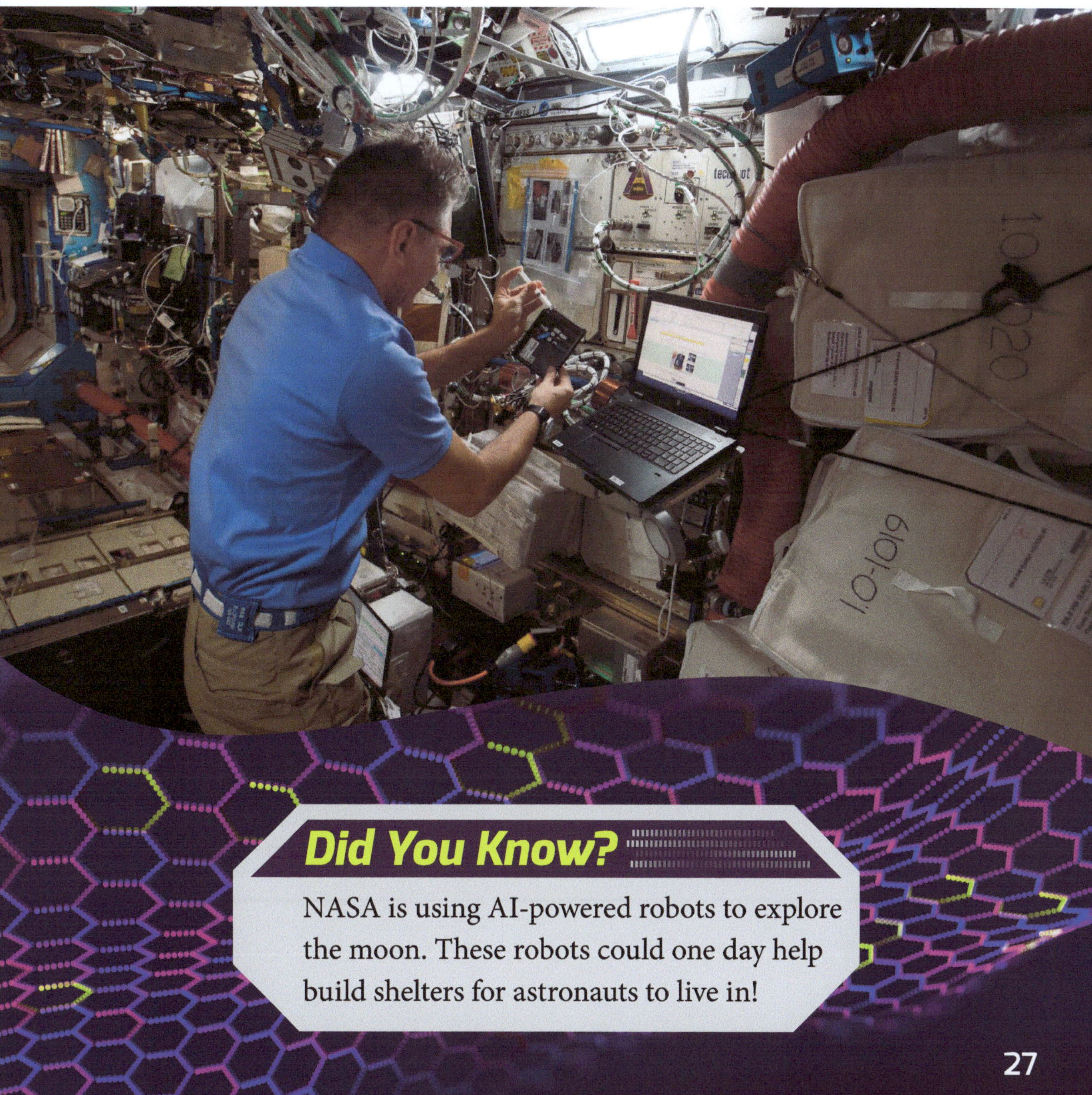

Did You Know?

NASA is using AI-powered robots to explore the moon. These robots could one day help build shelters for astronauts to live in!

AI is more than just smart machines. It's a tool that can help make the world better—for people, animals, and the environment.

It helps kids learn, supports doctors, protects wildlife, fights pollution, and even explores the stars. And there's more to come!

But with great power comes great responsibility. AI should always be used wisely. By learning how AI works, asking questions, and thinking critically, you can help make sure AI is used for good.

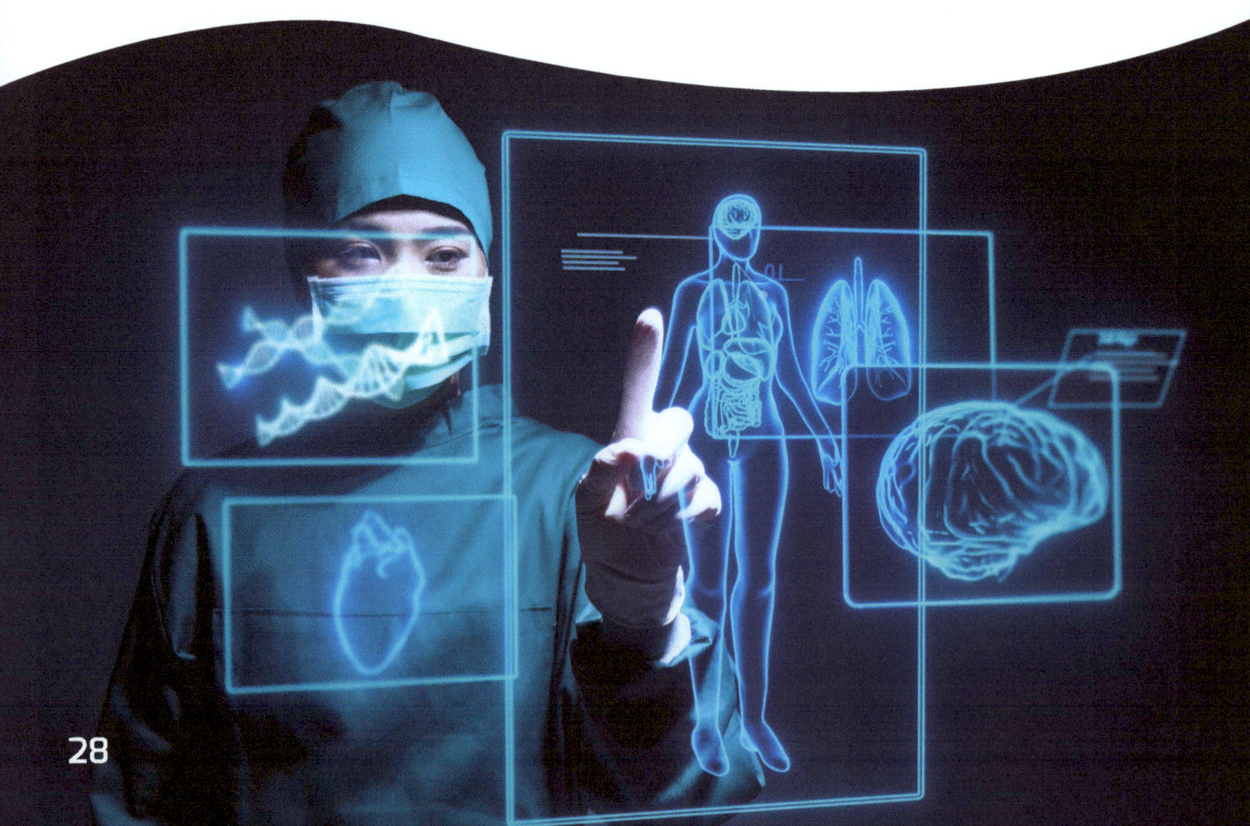

Be Smart About AI: Ask for Help

- Ask a parent or teacher for help when using AI technology.
- Stay curious and ask questions about the information AI provides.
- Remember: AI is a powerful tool and a big responsibility. Use it wisely!

Key AI Search Terms

1. AI for Kids
2. Artificial Intelligence Education
3. AI Learning Tools
4. AI in School
5. AI for Social Media Safety
6. AI and Privacy for Children
7. AI and Online Safety

Internet Sites

Britannica Kids: Artificial Intelligence
kids.britannica.com/kids/article/artificial-intelligence/390648

Code.org: Learning for Ages 5 to 11
code.org/student/elementary

ISTE: Artificial Intelligence in Education
iste.org/ai

Glossary

artificial intelligence (ahr-tuh-FISH-uhl in-TEHL-uh-juhns)—computers or robots that can think, learn, and solve problems like people

deforestation (dee-fohr-uh-STAY-shun)—the process of cutting down trees in forests, which can harm the environment

diagnose (DY-ig-nohss)—to figure out what's wrong with something, like when a doctor figures out what illness you have

endangered (in-DAYN-juhrd)—animals or plants that are in danger of disappearing forever

fertilizer (FUR-tuh-ly-zuhr)—a special substance that helps plants grow better and faster

poacher (POH-chur)—a person who illegally hunts or harms animals, often in a way that could hurt the species

pollution (puh-LOO-shuhn)—harmful things, like trash or chemicals, that can make the air, water, or land dirty and unsafe

satellite (SAT-uh-lyt)—machine that orbits the Earth or another planet; it collects information and sends it back to us

symptom (SIMP-tum)—a sign that shows you might be sick, like a cough or a fever

Index

About the Author

Tammy Enz holds a bachelor's degree in civil engineering and a master's degree in journalism and mass communications. She works as a structural engineer and teaches at the University of Wisconsin-Platteville. She has written dozens of books on science and engineering topics for young people.